Scouts are Cancelled

Annapolis Valley poems and one short story

Also by John Stiles

The Insolent Boy

Scouts are Cancelled

Annapolis Valley poems and one short story

John Stiles

INSOMNIAC PRESS

Edited by Paul Vermeersch
Copy edited by Adrienne Weiss
Designed by Mike O'Connor

National Library of Canada Cataloguing in Publication Data

Stiles, John D., 1966–
Scouts are cancelled : The Annapolis Valley poems and one short story / John Stiles.

ISBN 1-894663-25-X

1. Annapolis Valley (N.S.)--Poetry. I. Title.

PS8587.T554S36 2002   C811'.6   C2002-903814-6
PR9199.4.S75S36 2002

The publisher gratefully acknowledges the support of the Canada Council, the Ontario Arts Council and the Department of Canadian Heritage through the Book Publishing Industry Development Program.

Printed and bound in Canada

Insomniac Press
192 Spadina Avenue, Suite 403
Toronto, Ontario, Canada, M5T 2C2
www.insomniacpress.com

THE CANADA COUNCIL   LE CONSEIL DES ARTS
FOR THE ARTS   DU CANADA
SINCE 1957   DEPUIS 1957

ONTARIO ARTS COUNCIL
CONSEIL DES ARTS DE L'ONTARIO

For my mother, Victoria

To Cousin
Hillary,

Thanks for
having me
in 1986
and see you
soon, I
hope,

Love and
Best wishes

Morrissey's Headstone

Here lies Morrissey Wallis, 37
died one Serday, went to heaven
pinned under a tractor, late September
left wife, son, a farm, no daughter
loved he was by those that knew him
broad, some strong, tipped drops in bins
an orchard drunk, midnight singer,
one hard luck Gravenstein picker

Bernadette is some sly

Yes, Selma, he left me with a small house en a kid
en a dog en a man next door I hate most terrible

Yes, I seen em slinkin by in their small trucks
en I know they don't want no cleanin products
from me

But if you think I'm stupid, I'll remind you it was
you that loved Morrissey Wallis in high school.
You might be all set, Selma. But Bernadette Wallis
is still some sly.

Little Buggers my Mom

Little Buggers my mom said
to the three kids playin doctor
under the bushes

so she hiked up her skirt, took a rake
en poked at them en they run like chickens
through the lilac hedge

Erin held a goldfish in a Ziplock bag
en bawled her eyes oat on the porch

wall the dog drug its arse acrost the lawn

it was pissing down buckets

then Peter run like a flash past the house
en the window broke right side my head

My mom turned right around

you Big Bugger she yelled
at that dark-haired one

who had a garbage bag draped over his back like a cape
he was runnin like hell

through Mom's back garden with a margarine bucket
full of cucumbers, I imagine
he was fixin to trade fer dope

Dog Kennel
—for SPS

All six girls hung in the trees
like bats, pinafores en long white socks
they sang:

do re mi fa do

the boys in the sandbox pricked up
their ears

told the girls they were stupid, dug
holes deep as groundhogs

Mommy put clothespins in her mouth
bit hard en squeezed her fingers together:

underwear connected
to shirt connected
to socks connected
to the ol man's hankie

whin the boys was watchin
Mommy made a funny face

achooo

en blew
right off
the dog kennel she was stennin on

All She Wrote

Was in the kitchen with the fridge light on whin
I seen the ol feller from next door go by with his
head down, holdin onto a wheelbarrow fulla gourds

The cat was arfter him with his tail in the air en the feller
was holdin onto a hose en sprayin things all over hell's
half acre
> *kill this weed*
> *kill that weed*

En pitch gourds in the barrow

En then I seen his ol scritch wife in her nightie, her arse
look like two kids fightin under a blanket

She said when he was done sprayin them pear trees en gourds
was HIS FINE SELF ready to get back inside?

En whin he seen me glowin like a friggen strobe light, he stood
right up en said real stiff en embarrassed:

"Them tent caterpillers are droppin off them pear trees
like salt leeches off cousin Brenda at the Lumsden Dam
en that, my dear,
> is ALL SHE WROTE!"

En he set aboat clumpin back over his property in his gumboots
en his underwear, wearin an ol stringy hat

Don't need to tell you that I felt all weird when I seen the lights go off in their place, had to turn the volume button up on the TV even though I could hear nuthin goin down, Thank God

Her Kitty D.C.

That ol dog slunk right through the rhubarb, tail
between its legs en Peter's ball glove
innis mouth

damn thing was droppin in every hole
this side a the lilac hedge en my sister was cryin

cause her kitty D.C. (but I called him Spike) crawled
up into the cleanin ladies fan belt that arfternoon
en wandered in circles under the maple tree
before his eyes went cloudy en the cow flies
started their dive bomb

I threw a piece a slate at the dog, but my mom
was bangin at the window, fierce ol face on her

told me to bring my sister in, warsh are hands en eat
like we were supposed to, at the kitchen table

later on the steps goin up to are bedroom my sister
made a funny face

cause we heard are dad say he wished
it was Shep en not that Darned Cat that took
the fan belt like a bad kitty slap crost its
motorin little head

Ski-Doo Cord

Givver Jimmie Givver

Jimmie was all over that Ski-Doo like a Zellers T-shirt whin
Denny's hound poked her nose oat the dog kennel en made
sad eyes at him

ru ruuu ru ruuu

Denny held the window lock with his fingertips en wiped
his nose on his sleeve, his lips was blue like chrome

Siddown Ashley
Siddown on the rug

The dog bitched en chew her dog bowl tell it was like gum
Denny was acrost them bench seats, weasel face in the window

Givver Jimmie Givver

Jimmie shot straight up en backed
right into the corn

Runnnnnn Runmmmmmmmm Runnnnnnn Runnnnnnn nnnn nnn
nnn nnn

Denny threw his hand oat the car like a glove

Jesus, Mary, en Joseph, is that the dog er the Ski-Doo goin now?
Eh wha Milton?

Milton came back oat the cow corn holdin what looked
like a dead snake, grinnin like a shit eater

Had to get Jimmie's Ski-doo cord, he said
looks like the dog musta buried this little bitch in the cow corn
less spring

Not Far Behind
Big Black Dog

Major was his name, he was an ol dog with a pile
a grey en white whiskers, look like he stuck
his face in a fire

We all had a thing for that dog, even the smell a him
though he kinda waddled like a duck en whin I was small
I followed him through the fruit trees, the wild apples en
the firs en such

I saw my grandfather with that dog pullin him along
the ol dog had a limp en was thin en I knew then the ol man
had a big long stick with him with a bump on the end

He called it a sheleleigh, a stick with a bump,
bumped the stick on the dog's head, I seen it
with my own eyes

My mom had me in her lap en whin I seen my grandfather
go into the garage, get a spade, I said the dog's dead
en it was then my mom told me, the ol man's not far behind

Monkey's Island Song
—for CLB

[Riff/Stop]

Supper was done and we was oat the porch like we was
on fire er sumpin, bleedin from knees with carpenter ants
runnin up birch bark we fashioned inna canoes with moss en
Micmac braves with cow corn Barbie hair pasted on squaws
to tease the teacher in grade one

[1234]

the crick had eels innit en the cool one laid a string a wire
in the stream said he was gonna take a brook trout cause
it grew this long en we believed him cause his father
was a mean one anyways

[1234]

en are dad was stumblin oat the back with the dog bitin en
sniffin everything I mean are smart and totally clueless dad
callin the police cause he thought a body was buried where
ol Mrs. Demtouse grew her musharooms

[1234]

we was tiptoein acrost the cow paddies en upta Monkey's
Island trying to get Hodji to piss on the lectric fence wall we
piled under a lean-to playin doctor with the fat one

[bend]

then acted like angels in church on Sunday sittin cross-legged
beamin up at Jesus who looked sad when he wasn't lookin up
at the sky for sumpin he lost up there
in the friggen ol blindin sunshine

How Yah Doon a'night?

Jim en Rick er oat back, en Merle
is dummer 'n a sack fulla hammers

boys oh boys some folks never do learn
do they, now?

Bill Williams was at the Ox Pull Serday Night
dancin with Dick Spinney's wife

we all seen her bra
peach in colour

Eldon was on the picnic table
wearin his cut-offs

Craven A ugly
twist of a smile

you remember that young ferr
chisel-chin?
Wound his hockey stick up by his ear

sender back for a blapper
sender back for a blapper

drew KISS on his jeans in blue marker
en his mother drover school bus
right into the band room

you boys wanna spend the night in jail?
you boys wanna spend the night in jail?

or pick strawberries fer fifteen cents a quart?

they pay five en change fer drops
put em in buckets they salt the smelts in

[siren]

Scouts Are Cancelled

Jim Sutherland was a volunteer fireman
whin he wasn't are scout leader

he sure looked some stunned in a red tie
en brown slacks starin at a hall
a half-grown kids

so he rolled up his green sleeves, crouched down
en played crab soccer, kicked the ball hard
with a smoke innis mouth

Jim's mother warshed dishes at the strawberry suppers
en died of a stroke in the fruit trees oat back
left Jim a front porch fulla puppies
in a box with his winter coat

everyone who heard them guard dogs barkin
said it was such an awful shame

me and Lio used to collect tadpoles
in mason jars down at the village pond
en hold em right up to the sun

we were thinkin a tellin are mums we wanted
to quit scouts en join 4-H instead

wa wa wa wa
wa wa wa wa

whin the red fire trucks drove past we
set to smilin cause there wouldn't be cigarette
butts floatin like pond skippers in the toilet
bowl that set unner the church hall stairs

Lio, well, Elliot (Mason) Simpson

Elliot Mason is my name tho Mr. Simpson says I am Lio
like a Lion cause I should act more like a man

Mr. Simpson's got an opinion boat everythin, so I don't
say nuthin at dinner boat how come Mom don't go
by Mason no more nor talk boat my dad, Jerry Mason
who's a Lockeport lobster fisherman

So whin I get tense I make the funny faces that Selby likes
en try to stay oatta Mr. Simpson's hair

I weedle about in the fort that me en Selby made
in the apple crates oat back

One time I took my teddy up there en Selby tole me
to sit on em but I tole him to bring Erin's Ken doll cause
I wanted to show him how Mr. Simpson puts the blocks
to Mrs. (Mason) Simpson,

Um, yup, un huh, that's my mom

Trip up to the farm with the milk bucket

There was a ridge off the dykeland, down over
the grass en stink of the swamp where the eels
en rat bin: there was, at one time, a patch, look like
Mrs. Simpson poured hot water over ants

Was round en a little grassy with a little patch
a shirt, hung off the trees, belonged to Selby's
father whin he was alive

Been a tractor in these parts many many day ago
can't get through that patch now, too deep en filled
with broke bottles en the foundation of Bennie's trailer

Selby's ol man wouldn't have liked to see that trailer
down in that bog hole now (seen as he once tole me he
won that piece a land in a game a cards)

Alls I remember is Morrissey stalkin back from the
tavern with a two-four of Ten Penny up on his shoulders
like a big chip he wanted you to try to knock off

Day a Reckonin
Mr. Simpson

I'm a religious man. I was baptised in the Saint Peter's
Anglican Church like the resta you stunned fellers who
cuss my arse en make funna my Sunday suits. But I sold
this land fer Lio. I sold this land fer his mother en I'll
tell you now if I didn't do this some other feller with
a back hoe en no ties to this red clay would.

I still go to the Lions Club en chair the local Boy Scouts
pop bottle drive. I still smoke a little reefer. I used to
walk acrost that field whin I was a boy. I seen eagles
fly wide acrost the sky in my mind whin I'm alone.
Sweet Acres Subdivision. Acadian Bluegrass.
This here is my home, too.

Wide Load Sign
SWEET ACRES SUBDIVISION

[DRAMA] En then I seen Lio's friend, Maynard
[SETTIN IN] He had a small gun (BB, daisy, smoke)
he was talkin boat lobsterin with Mr. Mason in Lockeport
makin moran a month a Sundays than any us ever seen
in ten years a bailin hay

[MORE WITH RESOLVE]
En then the real quiet one who had glasses enna sore arse
from some friggen chrome disease said real slow en groany
like:

Yer goin downta Lockeport cause yer ol man
don't own the land yer trailer sets on en if yer lucky
you'll be rockin on the tossin sea en sick over the side
the same day they slappa big orinj WIDE LOAD sign
on the back truck that leaves yer place

en everyone'll cheer

whin they mow down em birch en poplars
en blackberry bushes en put in a subdivision
where yer cucumbers en pumpkins en gourds
rot en turn yellow cause a neglect

En then they'll put a sign on yer property that says
SOLD FOR COMMERCIAL DEVELOPMENT en sure
as shit they'll be friendly with one another in church
cause some contractor made money

tell there's talk a putting a crematorium

where the new development is gonna be
a small little shack where they can char to
cinders most anyone who keels over in their
rhubarb patch

en some poor feller in a Lions
meeting will be cussin cause we'll have houses
thrown up like gyprock, two goddamn bridges
over the Cornwallis River en cars killin family pets
all in the name a the new with the

Big Sign on the Highway

SWEET ACRES SUBDIVISION

Field a Ripe Pumpkins
—for Nathan

He was madder en all hell, cause he seen Selby's
mom in the window with a new red dress talkin
shop to Mr. Simpson

he was by that place many many times
with his ol feed truck, till he seen his ex-wife
pinched at the counter with Graydon's father

that set him right off, he was back at the family farm
in Canning,

in seconds flat he was takin a baseball bat
to a field a ripe pumpkins

Sweet Misery in the Grapevine
—for Phoebe

13-year-ol feller in a bust oat car, up back
en four fellers squashin minibikes like midget
Hell's Angels

that there "Sweet Misery" playin on the radio

Lio shouldna touched their beer, but he
did en so Graydon threw us over the reeds
en bullrushes, we had muddy arses
en nuthin moran

       two Ten Penny stubbies

which we set, with care and dignity, on the lip
a the grapevine

with the clock radio Lio stole, en my little sister
Erin was all quiet, listenin to "Sweet Misery" still
playin

Box Dis Ears

Was a meetin at the community centre
I sure as hell didn't go, but Lio wasn't oat back
er near are fort en the birds in the trees was as
silent as Christmas night

I seen Shep en I seen are cat en I seen all them cars
comin back from the Village like one big funeral
procession

I also seen Mr. Simpson go innis house en heard
him play bluegrass—near broke my eardrums whin
he started whistlin

I've never been a fighter, my mom taught me
to defend myself arfter school one day, hangin
Morrissey's hockey gear off the chin-up bar
in the hay barn

but whin I seen Lio settin on top the Simpson
Industries bulldozer I made a note in my head
right there en then

later in the night I woke up en I box dis ears
in my mind, moran jest one time

Aisle in the Co-op

Selma actually—
strange to see her cause she wasn't knittin er
gawkin oat the window at her friggen ol son
who was hidin in the woods, avoidin chores

she said, it was overheard, "We could use that money
to pay fer Carl's education, he has special needs, you know?"

then she bustled down the fifth aisle with her
list lookin fer skim milk powder, dates en lard fer home baking

this was some shocker, cause it was Selma who made her
Sunday school class sing
"This land is yer land" at the St. Peter's Parish picnic

Selma who stood like a preacher on the cliffs
a the Minas Basin sayin
we'd all go to hell in a handbasket if we ever
let go a this here salt-tide red-stink land

Got Some Nerve
Overheard at the Women's Institute Meeting

"Oh my Lamb.
Now will he pave over the Bay a Fundy, too?"

Em Moody Days

Down in the friggen ol mire in the black stinky ol mud
a the pond with the oil in puddles I was makin rainbas

whin I look at the
                    SWEET ACRES SUBDIVISION
sign

I don't mind it so much cause the bulldozer ploughed over
that ol dump en at least we don't have to look at dead chickens
hangin from trees en eggshells all scattered over like chickets

but (course, right?)

whin my mom sees me as I come in she says you're havin
one a yer moods again en she puts away the box a cleanin products
she's trying to huck to the next door neighbour en it gets all quiet en
even the cats, never mind the dog, find reason to go en hide behind
the sofa again

Selby's Prayer

Dear Lord in Heaven I think aboat girls in school
en me havin invisible powers so I can watch them
take a bath. Does that make me a bad man?

Dear Lord in Heaven I can't sit still in Sunday
school er be nice to Lio at recess er tell Bernadette
I almost shoplifted at recess. Does that make
me a bad man?

Dear Lord sometimes I think that Morrissey
can see me up in heaven and he knows
I get depressed en do that lonely thing
in the bathroom. Does that make me a bad man?

Dear Lord in Heaven I jest want to be with
Bernadette en have her be the way she was
when I was four en Mo was still a speck
en so that's exactly what we called him—Speck.

Sometimes I don't wanna get another day wiser
en I think a joinin my dad,
(you know where he is, right?). Does that make me
a bad man?

Tide Are In (fer Gossips)
—for DAS

The hockey coach crouched over the court report cause
the Glenville Wildcats goalie was late fer practice again

The butcher dropped *The Advertiser* in his bucket
a slop cause that famous sour-faced painter wandered
into the L.C. en snubdum (did you see him at the Post Office
in them wraparound shades?)

En little missy-elementary-school-whatserface read
that when the school burnt down there was that bald
scientist from Horton's Landing up there on the top
a the Fire Truck wavin the boys on

—whisper poetry—

no mention of The Subdivision at all,
now that feller drinks coffee with ol Jeff Pick
the fire chief went to Harvard on a scholarship
comes from some place called Crousetown
on the south shore ain't nothing there but wind
even when the tides are comin back in en drown
oat the sound a crows en folks yellin
down the sand dunes at their kids who're
sittin in the mud diggin fer poisoned clams

Bike, No Hands

Them pigeons set on the Shur Gain towers
like small en silent kings, tell a bald eagle
come wide through the sky en spooked em right under
the Cornwallis Bridge

Down below was Lio, he was onnis bike, kinda windin,
no hands, through the nits en bugs en whatnot
(said they look like lint in the sunlight) he was goin
arfter a cat en the cat slunk through the crates

Someone was yellin *Jesus H. Karist* there's rat
poison there, you'll skid on that feed

Lio still went this way en that tell he seen
that eagle pass over like a cloud en he went
right over the pier, inna the muck

The kids teased him sumpin fierce:
had to get a three wheeler down there
with a chain

The sound he made comin oat was sumpin
terrible, like pullin a dirty foot
oat a gumboot, I guess

(it was *gluuuuuschhhht*)

Kipawo Showboat Feller

Me en Lio in are scout uniforms walkin
slow en solemn behind the Lions
Community Float

Princess Berwick, done up some nice,
perched on a Towne Car side some fool
from Valley Stationers grinnin

En a school band from Gaspereau
poor little retards like silvery fishes

Queen Annapolisa stuck up on the 4-H tractor
like sumpin oatta Guys en Dolls

Shriners on scooters with the grand
pooh-bah wavin sumpin

There goes Dandee Apple, arms skinny
as lectrical cord, with his tatty ol tuxedo
en big Apple Head
walkin lonely into the Glennville ballpark

En the Kipawo Showboat feller with the RCMP

Wall on the side, a pile a grubs in fold up chairs
en cigarettes danglin like lengths a log

One is
eyein the Kipawo Showboat Feller
like he jest might have sumpin on him

Lot 4 Sale, Haligonian?

It sits there like a big flower plate
a meadow with a tractor, nearly broke down,
the way they talk is peculiar, they seem
nice, cautious, I suppose

(I'll put four bathrooms in, pave the drive,
landscape the lot...)

I felt this way about my own land on the South
Shore when the Americans come in the *sumah*
from *Booah*

That funny Maine talk like a quiet
damp stink on a porch

All this land is sun, the sun shines off
Canaan Mountain, these people don't know
that I'll just come in on weekends

They won't catch me down at Bills Lunch
for more than bread, though I like that store,
looks like a picture postcard from my winter
trips down to *Buckspawt* in the *sumahtime*

Frig That Shit
Bills Lunch Notice Board

Bunnies 4 Sale.
Lio Simpson you get right home!!
Scouts are cancelled.
Strawberries available at Varney's U-Pick.
Bring your own containers.
Tuba. With case. Dents.
The Village Stripper has relocated to the Country Fair Mall.

Record of a tractor

Chains on them wheels like
the sound of ox bells, cept different

can't abuse a tractor like you can oxen
specially when they won't pull, my Jeez

did you know that Mr. Sheffield
lost one eye to cancer, poked the other
oat in the orchard

he was up there with them cats, did you know
the sound a a tractor
is like the sound of a cat purrin

so many cats in the hay barn

can't find nuthin in the dark now
oh my Jeez

Torpedo Chicken
—for the Sinjer

Scrawnie Rawnie was an ol time
stun a mun, hair like a musharoom
standen stiff in flood jeans

His ol lady drover school bus en his brother drove
his minibike right through Mr. Simpson's cherry trees,
on his weekend pass from Waterville County Jail

Scrawnie Rawnie answered 'n ad in *The Advertiser*
year arfter year:

There's four to a cage en yah drop
the roosters on the floor, ten cents
on the dollar
for every one you don't hurt

Holdin that newspaper en chewing a half
packa Hubba Bubba, Scrawnie Rawnie looked into
that pile a wire cages with beaks stickin through

Best get down to 'er Rawnie said the farmer, toppa
his tractor en tippin his sunglasses, watchin a young
hen run hard fer the corn

Don't like chickens much do yah Rawn?

my friend Lio yelled as Rawnie watched us kids
flippin hockey cards under the maple tree
in the friggen hot ol sun

Truth be told I can't stand em

Rawnie grumbled, but he got right quiet whin Eldon
give him a rope burn so he took the double decker
tell nearly every one was in

feathers flew en grunts en mumbles en us kids sat
cross-legged while the farmer laid out two crisp ten-dollar
bills in Rawnie's hand

Pop bottle money

said Scrawnie Rawnie to the three a us
sidden in are scout uniforms
in a cloud a dust below the truck

En hockey card money
said Eldon

we all watched Scrawnie en Eldon drivin unsteady
on back a a minibike, down a dirty dust road

Torpedo Chicken

called my friend Lio when the farmers hound chased
that same young white hen en it flew back oat the cow
corn en settled down on Rawnie's head like she was layin a
egg on him

Chip Factory Foreman

Maynard was a dope smoker, wore a blue GWG jacket
he draped over Rhonda's shoulders, his fat arsed
girlfriend, my friend Lio called her *Spawnicow*

Maynard never liked me much, but I never took shit
from him even whin I was beatin him at Pac Man
en he was pokin me with hands en had

Rhonda done Maynard

scribbled all over in jet-black ink

Waca Waca Waca Waca Waca Waca Waca
Waca Waca Waca Waca Waca Waca Waca

Cherry (*woop*) Strawberry (*woop*) Banana (*woop*)

Paper route money went on video games, allowance
on dirty magazines, the guidance counsellor told my
mom I was jest a lazy port rat headed straight fer
vocational school

Waca Waca Waca Waca Waca Waca Waca
Waca Waca Waca Waca Waca Waca Waca

Extra man (God Damn!)

Whin the noon bell rung we all run back
acrost the New Minas Road with handfuls a licorice
en half moons en carmel cakes en a can a Dr. Pepper

Maynard had a bag a Dill Pickle chips fer Rhonda
who like I said had the pantylines en a big fat arse
en an eye fer other men

Up the stairs we all run, set like a bunch a poor fellers
in back a boring maths class, wall the teacher broke
his chalk on the board

I stared oat the window
watched all the pretty girls playin lob ball with
the bull-dyke who taught phys. ed class

What you boys wanna be? asked the teacher
we all said *College Graduates*, except fer Maynard
who stuffed his face with chips en said

Chip Factory Foreman

Rhonda laughed en pinched Maynard's arse en
I counted the money I took off him en watched
him rub her titties, harder at the lockers at the end
a maths class

What you lookin at Selby? (asked Maynard)
en I said his money

but Maynard had the last laugh cause he seen me sittin
in backa the detention late bus munchin on stale licorice
all sullen en spiteful:

see I didn't have no girlfriend, didn't take my skin
tell the end a grade ten

Trapped Fly?

Billy Olfield slouched in back a home ec
class buzzing like a trapped fly

Pretty much all the fellers in that hot room
hadda hate on fer him, cause he wore glasses taped
in the middle en beat at his lips sumpin fierce

"Weird how he started doon that, eh," said
the one girl who wasn't in metal shop

"Weird how he jest watches us in the parking lot
when he stoops down to pick up em Peter
Stuyvesants er Export As."

"Well I pissed him off once," said Rona. "Gottan A
in my industrial arts test en alls I had fer him
when he bummed a smoke off me was a tube a
orchard peach lipstick, a pack a wet matches
en that ashtray I ground too hard on the lathe."

Rocket on the Dykes

My friend Donnie hadda thing fer fuses, parachutes,
gunpowder en matches. He'd light a flint, burnis hands
jest so he could run down the dykes en tell his mom

sky is fallin
sky is fallin
sky is fallin

So whin I seen the plastic action figure head down
in the muck, I knew Donnie was oat on the dykes
someplace, he could tell the size en distance of a model
rocket engine cannister jest by squeezin it

Christ he was obsessed with the BIG MISSILES:
a whole army a silent men, hangin down from
Gravenstein trees with stars all over their parachutes
powerless

Bang bang bang said Donnie
layin in the grass

Looks like a slug in shorts a girl in back a the bus
said when she seen him wrigglin on his belly through
all that stinkin silage

He was always in the window at the local Zellers
when we was playin Missile Comand er buyin lures.

He wasn't innerested in fishin

I always liked the shiny Mepps or the Black Fury

en dippin my rod in the Cornwallis River
(tell I nearly fell off the pier
whin I seen that slimy Safeway bag
with dead kittens inside)

Donnie was oat there on his tractor
dark as all hell, flickin his Bic lighter

We was layin in bed thinkin of are trip to Disneyland
now there was a Remax SOLD sign
on are front lawn like a tombstone

Was sumpin in the air I guess

We all stood durin "Oh Canada"
for a moment a silence for Donnie,

who they said needed three doctors
with pliers to pry his new shirt from Zellers
en that big Saturn rocket
oat the centre of his chest:

his face was white as a sheet they said but
in his hands was one a them action figures
with the Kung Fu Grip

Glennville Hospital Walkathon

Strung along the road like gulls from yoho
we watch em, poor folk from the local dump
canvassin fer the Glennville Hospital Walkathon

One in a bomber jacket, name a Edna,
lay on the train tracks cause she was
depressed whin she come home from the Harold
Fuller Travelling show

She's in cadets now, carryin
some Ontario carnie's kid

Elmer Smale, rake thin, had Barry Almond
up on the ruff a his trailer with a ball-peen
hammer cause Barry's wife give him dirty looks
in church, one too many times

The fat one goes along, you try to yell at him,
pick on him, cause kids er mean, actually they are
all quite miserable to the yoho

tell some hysterical white-faced fruity
boy leans from his door and yells *I love you*

en so we all get tense fer a moment
en turn are bile on him

Ferris Wheel Carnie

Three fer a kawtah, John Fawtah,

The fat kid nursed his lolly en fought with a yellow rain-
coat that cocooned him

wall the Ferris Wheel Carnie, black-billed cap en fiery
burns grunted: *it's four tickets fer a ride, nut two*

en some smart arse Acadia kid said *that feller looks
like a cross between Ronald McDonald en Satan*

en the announcer lowered himself in his booth

*All Set All Paid Ready To Go Where She Stops
Nobody Knows* en the carnie said:

Four Tickets I Said, Nut Two

en that fat kid started to bawl when he saw the
Ferris Wheel get goin, he saw his sister raise right up
jest a little ways

her hair was stuck in the gears en the brakes made
a sound like a train en that ol carnie went arfter
her with a pair a scissors glintin in the sun

her mother screamed en held her as she sat white-faced
a little blood like a candy apple bite
in the hand of the carnie who—I seen it—stooped
to kiss her fer a whistle-stop second

Annapolis Valley Radio
Broadcast News Report

Sunk right into the bed lookin at a manual aboat how to fix the
hair drier that's now busted, yer world is a thirteen-year-old
world en yer hair, yer beautiful Farrah Fawcett-style hair
that the girls like is all brushed into the corner in the kitchen
with the rest a the compost en yer mum is singin too loud, uh huh

Still the feller on the radio, on Annapolis Valley Radio, is jest a
givvin er aboat the lots they got fer sale in the new
SWEET ACRES SUBDIVISION

en yer tryin not to worry aboat it cause you know that the
girl you played spin the bottle with in band class most
likely is goin to be pressed hard into Jimmie Oldsman
or Ed Banks en not you cause you got your hair all cut

En you—as you lay there beneath the sheets—you look like you
should be signed up weth the reserves in Aldershot even
though you know if there was a war you'd be this side
a useless standin there, ignorin the sergeant en listenin
to yer little pocket radio fer General Hand Grenade er at least
quotin the slow part on the AVR"Broadcast Neeeeeews Report."

A Thousand Fleas

Them two Mills boys was wearin socks pulled up
round their ears en they said to the tall feller
lookin at a jar a plum conserve

they said do you like that en the tall man said I do en the kid
said I hate it en the man said why's that now en the other
kid said he's the difficult one

en then the table come down en their ol lady come arfter them
with a length a switch, the littlest one said to the gawkin
man with the Remax sign under his arm, he said: May
A Thousand Fleas Infest Your Armpits, Sir.

Fer the Pardy

I'll tell you right now I ain't innit fer the pardy
er the girls that look atcha like they wanna piece
a sumpin er sumpinerudder, right?

En arfter yer done you feel like the man from the Insurance
companies been round whin jest three seconds ago
you was sinkin into the couch talkin to the cats
like they was ol friends

En right there on the porch is a girl in a slip lookin atcha
like she wants a little piece a sumpin er sumpinerudder, right?

Jesus girls are meaner'n boys with bats on baseball
diamonds I was thinkin that whilst I was lyin on my bed watchin
cow flies I think we called them blue boddles whin I was a kid

Hah Hah Hah the jokes are all fine
till yer stuck in the room with one a em

Seems like the girls ain't as innocent as yer mom
who'll come in from pickin apples, hike up her skirt
tell you you was late fer bed again
whilst you set there in the bath, tryin not to look

Tubin?

You boys ain't goin Tubin, not in that stink water
it's no moran three degree farenheit if I'm forty years a day

see I might have a grade six education en be unemployed
two years come September but I quit drinken
four years ago come this Apple Blossom Parade

nope

you boys ain't goin Tubin
not till you pay fer that conveyor belt Jimmie Sandford
bent right in half up on Deep Hollow Road

Now what it was doon there I jest don't know

If I was you fellers I'd take that mickey a rye en swing
from the Gaspereau Bridge

cause that there murky river yer lookin at
is full a beer bottles en broken cars

know why I know?

I once stood the top a Murphy's corner
with Jimmie Sandford's father, we torched
the Hortonville school bus
senter right down Wallbrook Mountain

the whole Annapolis Valley lit right up like a bonfire
en the town sirens went right wild

now that was Halloween night '77
wall we was still on probation fore these snot-nosed kids
come in the house en left me singin on the cold
lonely porch
with the dog bitin at her sores

nope

you fellers ain't goin Tubin not if I still got
my sixteen gauge shot gun en a bag a rock salt
that'll make yah yip like this here dog

less Tuesday night

whin she chased my prize Dutch rabbit
right oat her hutch
with Jimmie Sandford

set like a fat Mallard duck right in the goddamn
dunk tank
at the Berwick County Volunteer
Fireman's Fair

Wolfville Ridge Road
Selby's Dream?

Turnin the wheel thisaway then thattaway
thisaway then thattaway

en you hit that pedal
like 140 ain't nothin

yer goin along
thinkina Lynn thinkina Lynn goin along en drivin
drivin like you gotta get home before one
but its already four

Lynninthacar Lynninthacar
parked in the driveway en
Lynninthacar inner white cotton shorts

en you kiss en you kiss en you kiss

yer goin along thinkina Mom thinkina Mom
cannen beetroots in the kitchen
all white inner face en madatcha
cause yer a fool fer girls
en maybe she's one uv em

goin along en drivin
drivin like you gotta get home
before one but it's already four

Yer mom in the backyard
givvin it to you, it's
nothin to be proud a, yer attitude en state a mind

what a waste a life
you dumb stupid child

goin along
en drivin, drivin like you gotta get home
before one but it's already four

Them words Lynn said. In them shorts. In yer car.
I'm boy crazy little fellah. I'm boy crazy.
En you hit the pedal, up over 160

en that was Lynn with F_____ at the cinema
cause she's boy crazy en she's sixteen
en yer seventeen

turnin the wheel
thisaway then thattaway thisaway then thattaway

goin along
en drivin, drivin like you gotta get home
before one but it's already four

Light up ahead lonely
house on the Wolfville Ridge Road

You hear the tires
they go so loud you don't care if yer dead er alive
till the sparks en a car passin light you up
as you pull out the window en stumble down the road
with dogs barkin

it's slo mo en
you see yer face in the mirror a the window

a the ambulance en it's your uncle tellin you
You'll never leave the house again

yer goin along
en drivin, drivin like you gotta get home
before one but it's already four

so you stiff yer uncle for any feelins
en creep oat the house
en you drive up along the Wolfville Ridge Road
with a can a beer
like yer married er sumpin
with yer lil Lynn singin at yer side
en yer honkin the horn at that lonely house
drivin past
in yer uncle's new family car

Blackberry Bushes

Up back we went me en my mom en the blackberries was all bluey like a friggen ol bruise en we was in are shorts down by Scotty's fort en in by the crick with shotgun casins like markers squashed flat in the reeds en muck

We was puttin them berries in the ice cream buckets en talkin boat the Second World War en her ol man oat there standin proud en certain in the cold French wind

En we was talkin about secrets a woman has en I was tryin not to bitch en complain too much about things cause I was wearin shorts oat there en my mom—when she wasn't hummin en worryin about my little sister— my mom was cryin occasionally

En I was asking her if it was her finger or legs that took a scratch like a cat en she said no you bloody damned boy it's your father or her father, the one in the war, en so I fought through the wild cucumbers en picked away at a bush a blackberries while she went off blamin my ol man aboat this or that

En I put them bluey blackberries in the ice cream bucket en they looked like blood there, that's what I tole my mom anyways en she tole me that I shouldn't be so damned melancholy or sumpin en I tole her that I loved her en she tole me that she loved me en that I was the special one but that sometimes the special one wasn't the wanted one at certain times

Scotty's Fort

Jesus you'd think the boys'd plan better'n buildin an
ugly clapboard fort right under the shiny runoff from the
chicken barn all tangled in with the wild cucumbers en
birdocks

Jesus you'd think the school would have the good sense
nut to pile into that dank ol shack confessin loves fer one
another whin they won't say hello in French class whin
they pass each other in pinchy North Stars in the hall-
ways a Horton High

it was that flashlight through the night en all those kids
filin oat a that shack like rats oat the sewers with the
farmer leadin the way on top a his tractor

I was sure they all thought it was me tole him boat the
stupid pardy at Scotty's fort but it wasn't me it was that
girl from French class who wasn't allowed oat in the
evenins en was stuck in music class most the time, starin
oat the window, pinin

Rabbit Through Snow

Bennie's stuck on Darla but she ain't comin down
off Caanan mountain tell they plum that ol house
en layya string a wire oat back

I never seen shit piled up but I do know what
an oathouse looks like tipped over—
looks like a rabbit runnin through the snow

Jest another subdivision with lots priced at 45
en a good piece a land with houses thrown
up like Lego

There used to be apple trees there, a Captain's house
en a steam ship that come in from Volstovny fer pulp

but now alls I see in that there ol Gravenstein acreage
is a SOLD sign stamped like a red bruise en a black en
white rabbit hoppin across the white cotton snow lettin
turds fall where they may, where they may

Me en Lio

Down home folks used to call me dumb ol Selby cause I'd rather stand by the winda en crush cow flies gainst the pane then play four square in the playground with a buncha hollerin kids. Lio Simpson was the worst a them ferrs yellin in the schoolyard cause he was supposed to be my best friend. Elliot Simpson was his real name though he'd tell all the pretty girls it were Lio. Sometimes we'd be lyin on the porch readin skin magazines en he'd whisper, "My stepfather tole me that when your mom soaks in the bathtub she looks jest like that one there with the curly hair."

Alls I remember boat them days is that I was mad most days. If I tole you I used to ride my dad's ol motorbike on the dykes en pick up pop bottles that I found in the crik you might not think that was too strange. But the two ol ferrs from the Canada Packers Plant thought I was a retard or some damn thing. Soon as I showed up at the convenience store some kinda weird silence'd sweep over the place. I'd tie Shep to the ice cooler en go in through the screen door en Fulton Rushton'd have his elbows on the counter en he'd be talking like he didn't see me settin there. He'd be goin, "That dumb kid, Selby Wallis. Boy forgot to stop at the Petro Can en I seen him pushing that little dirt bike back over the Cornwallis Bridge with a gas container in his henns lookin to git some gas." En Sheldon Gates, who was dumber n a sack full a hammers nod n agree with him.

"Did he have the limpin dog with him, Fulton?" He'd go. En Fulton'd make that there *Hmmm Hmmm* sound en then Fulton'd turn right around. He'd push his glasses up his nose. "Well, now Selby Wallis. How you doon aday?"

"Mumma's jus' fine." I'd say looking away from them. Then I'd pay fer the licorice en the gobstoppers with the 7Up bottle I found in the crick on the way down.

Oh-my-jumpins.
Oh-my-lamb.

Our next door neighbour Selma used to chit-chat like that all the time. She'd be set on a stool cradlin the receiver to her ear, knittin, en she'd take the phone away from her mouth en say, "Lio your mom says she don't want you boys goin up back a'night. They bin spreadin manure on the cow corn en we'd both like you boys round here where we can keep an eye on yahs."

Course, me en Lio never listened to what ol fat arse was sayin anyways. We'd sneak up back as soon as she was on the phone again en climb the big red silo en pull are boots off en jump down into the wet mess a cow stalks en squish the hot silage between are toes. Whin we were done up there we'd race up to the hay barn en make forts en tunnels en talk some aboat the girls. Selma'd be ready for us whin we got home, though. She'd be stennin there in the screen door watchin us wade through the quack grass to get the green shit off are boots en she'd yell at us en say she was gonna take a birch switch cross the back of are legs cause she'd caught her own young ones perched on the lip a the silo like pigeons, lookin to jump off.

"You go on, Shep."
"Git now."
"Git home."

Lio's stepfather used to yell at Shep all the time cause are stupid three-legged hound dog was always pissin on his cherry trees en tomatus. Mr. Simpson used to throw rocks arfter Shep too en the stupid dog'd come home hoppin en puffin, hoppin en puffin, en then he'd drop into a hole under the lilac bushes en sniff a little bit at the ground. Course, Mr. Simpson'd be right polite whin he seen the pretty school teacher acrost the street walkin *her* dog. He'd smile whin she'd call over to him.

"Beautiful evenin' isn't it, Merle?"

En he'd go, "It sure is." En then he'd put his henns up near his face, tip his softball cap en take a big lazy golf swing arfter her.

"Git, Shep. Git."
"Git home."

I always knew Lio en Mr. Simpson never got along on
account of the way Lio acted whin we was playin softball
in the summertime. There'd be a crowda dirty-faced kids
stennin over home plate en Lio'd always be last to go
before the girls. Lio'd scrunch up his face en walk, bow-
legged, over to the snotty little girl from acrost the way.
He'd go, "My arse jest grunted your name, Brenda. What
in hell's half acre do you have to say to that?"

But Brenda, who was the town dentist's daughter,
would be ready for him whin he come up like a big dark
shadow. "Close your legs, Elliot Simpson, yer breath
stinks," she'd say. En then she'd poke her nose further
into her colourin book. En jest then whin everyone was
all loose laughin, Mr. Simpson'd show up on the veran-
da acrost the way en sten there with his henns folded
acrost his chest watchin the diamond where we was
playin. En I could tell from lookin at Lio, cause he'd be
stennin at the plate bitin his bottom lip, that he'd be
watchin Mr. Simpson oat the corner a his eye the whole
time.

The thing boat Mr. Simpson was I couldn't take my eyes
off him whin he was around. It wasn't that he was big or
nothin. It was more in the careful way he moved, en the
way he chose his words, sumpin serious aboat him that
said: everythin I do is aboat bein a man. He always
seemed real quiet when he was oat with his wife at one
of the Strawberry Suppers or at the Village Ox Pull or

one a the craft fairs. He always kinda trailed behind her wall she looked over at the brown bread or the rhubarb pies on the bake table, henns behind his back, maybe, sometimes whistlin.

I used to get real mad at Lio cause Mr. Simpson used to take Lio deer huntin oat in Musquoidobit en Lio always used to whine sayin he didn't *wanna* go deer huntin oat in a dirty ol stinky swamp with mosquitoes en sink holes en bats swoopin down on him en whin Lio talked like that I near strangled him cause he didn't know how lucky he was to have the chance to go. But if Lio hated goin deer huntin, he sure loved goin fishin. Every year around the end a April him en his stepfather go jiggin for smelts under the Melanson Bridge near where the Gaspereau curves oat towards the Minas Basin. Lio'd follow in behind Mr. Simpson, wearin gumboots, holdin a big white bucket, en they'd be down there on the muddy banks a the Gaspereau River castin lines into the dark rushin tides.

I always knew me en Lio had are differences but I never knew it was cause a cats en dogs. Cat people en dog people are different the way I see it now. Dog people like their driveways filled with half-tons en like to play loud bluegrass music on their verandas, in the summertime. Cat people like quiet radio music en set down on porches, not verandas, en their houses are kinda dirty. Plates pile up in the sink fer days en dirt gets swept inna corners en the porch stinks a cat pee en the furniture is all rough en fuzzy en the wallpaper peels off walls cause the cats are always layin on their backs en scratchin on it. Now are ol three-legged hound dog wasn't no cat neither but Shep musta thought he was cause instead a pissin on are porch he liked to piss on Mr. Simpson's garden plants.

"Git, Shep. Git."
"Git home."

The reason I know all a this is cause a Lio. The Simpsons had that rich folks house with the paved driveway, the veranda, the nice paint job en the two black Labs that always barked at Shep whin he was over there sniffin en pissin. Lio used to say, "Why don't you drown some a them barn cats en take a shotgun to that damn three-legged mutt a yours?"

"The ol lady," I said tryin to sound tough. "The ol lady wouldn't like that, Lio." Then Lio made a funny face en picked his ear.

"Shep's a dog, not a cat, Selby."

"Shep don't act like a dog," I yelled back. En I flung a pile a cat shit arfter him.

The reason we had so many cats was cause Ma had a thing for strays. My daddy always used to say that was why Ma liked him so much, cause she didn't know where he came from en didn't know when he'd up en leave, en that's why she put up with him hidin oat in the garage till all hours a the night with his bottle a apple cider singin en carryin on late into the evenin. Ma'd be layin in the soapy bath water with the damned door open so I could

see her from my bedroom where I'd listen to the water
slop in the tub, en I'd be listenin to that en my drunk ol
man out there cursin en singin en whistlin.

One evenin, Ma gave Lio a cookie, a fresh baked
molasses cookie, en he said somethin to her that day
made me start to hate him. "Did you wash yer henns
before you baked that cookie Mrs. Wallis?" he asked her.
En my, ma cause she couldn't help it, wiped her henns
acrost the backa her nose en then wiped it on her apron
en said, "Lio that's mean talkin like that, jest plain
mean."

But Lio never was scared a my ma. He laughed in a
goofy way en said, "I'm jest askin, Mrs. Wallis, I'm jest
askin."

En my ma paused for a moment all hurt en said,
"Who's been talkin Lio, who who's been sayin stuff
Lio?" en then I got on him some myself.

"Yah who you been sayin stuff Lio?" En finally he
said, "It's jest a bad habit is all, Mrs. Wallis. Mr. Simpson
says nose pickin's a real dirty habit."

I named my cat Mo after that same crazy drunken dad a
mine, Morrissey Wallis, who died the year arfter I turned
four. Morrisey Wallis was pickin drops in Varney's Apple
Orchard whin the tractor he'd left idlin up the hill rolled
down en pinned him unner a big ol Gravenstein tree. En
though he's dead now the whole village still talks aboat
my dad like he's some kinda legend cause whin he was
younger he liked the tavern too much. Course, his dyin
only added to that legend cause the day before he died he

picked a Varney's Orchard record: Nine en a half bins a bruised up, brown en rotten Gravensteins.

Mo was a orange coloured tom cat with long white scratches on his underside en head, en who always had a smell boat him like musk. I used to hold him in my arms en bring him onto the porch, en he'd jest lie on the floor wall I tried to stuff his paw into an empty beer bottle or catch his tail under the phone book. He'd always jest roll over on his back en start purrin en thumpin his tail gainst the dusty wood floor, en I used to whisper in his ear how he had the spirit in him a my dead dad.

Well, it came oat through the doorway of their veranda, en when I heard it the first time, I wasn't sure it was real. It sounded like TV or sumpin the way the words were goin en I remember thinkin it was *Charlie's Angels* tell I heard the "smack" en the sobbin, real quiet, that followed.

He ain't nothin but a damn liability, Carol, he never listens to a goddamned thing I say. How am I supposed to be a role model fer your son, if he don't even listen to what it is I'm sayin? Groundin him for bein bad ain't the answer, Carol, you gotta make him understen. You ask me, he's gone a little queer. He likes playin house more than he likes playin softball with the neighbourhood kids, en he likes that retard Selby from acrost the way. Well, if you weren't...

en then I heard the second "smack." I only heard it the two times, but there I was walkin up back through the dennylions en skinny chokecherry trees with Mo. But I soon dropped the cat oat a my arms cause I was pluggin my ears with my henns.

Shep got hit by Mr. Simpson's truck that same summer bouta month before school got goin again. Shep was off his chain as usual stoppin en sniffin, stoppin en sniffin when he hopped across the baseball field en right in back of Mr. Simpson's half-ton. The dog let out a bad sound en he was pantin for a long time arfter his eyes got all watery en runnin. I remember Mr. Simpson gathered him up into his arms en brung him over to are porch sayin to Ma, "I'm so sorry Mrs. Wallis for what has happened here." Right then he lay ol Shep down on the front porch, en the dog kicked a little en there was blood on his grey whiskers en his ears were pulled backwards showin the pink en yellow stuff inside. My ma had trouble breathin, I think, cause she was makin a funny sound. "He was such a good company, Mr. Simpson, we'll probably never gonna get us such a good hound like that again." En I was proud a her when she said that. She didn't whimper, or ask him to get her a new dog or nothin, she just brushed off her henns on her apron en walked inside en closed the screen door when she was done with Mr. Simpson en what it was she was sayin.

Mr. Simpson musta felt bad for ol Shep cause that same arfternoon he wrapped the dog in a sheet en took him to a wood pile that the pheasants used to hide in up back. Lio came with us en seemed real quiet watchin the hole gettin dug en watchin the body gettin lowered down into it. A couple a times Mr. Simpson tole Lio that he had half a mind to bury Lio in that hole with Shep, en when he said that it was all I could do not to laugh cause Lio was bitin hard on his lower lip. Then arfter Mr. Simpson finally left, me en Lio stood there all alone. En I wasn't sure if Lio was gonna say sumpin smart er sumpin stupid, en alls I knew was that I hated Lio bein there with me. En Mo, a course, came runnin from the compost pile en started rubbin up under my legs purrin en lookin up at me. So I crouched down en scooped the cat up into my arms en stood there solemn like, scratchin under the cat's neck.

Right then Lio started tryin to take the cat oatta my arms, en I was holdin Mo en pattin him en tryin to hold him back away from Lio.

"Gimme the cat for a sec," said Lio. Then he started whinin arfter a bit. "I wanna hold him is all, Selby."

En I said "no" in a real calm voice.

En Lio grabbed a handful a wild cucumbers offa the vine en started peltin them arfter me.

"I ain't gonna hurd it, Selby."

Course, with Lio throwin like a girl the wild cucumbers went flyin by en so I stuck my tongue oat at Lio en started walkin back down towards the porch.

"My dad hates that cat, Selby," yelled Lio. "My dad's half-ton's gonna lay that cat flat."

"At least my daddy loved me," I said as I was walkin back down the hill scratchin the cat's neck. En I don't know why I said it. It wasn't right me sayin what I said but it felt pretty good anyways. En right then I looked back over my shoulder en I seen Lio standin there shiverin, his face all white, en I looked down at the green spiky cucumbers fallin on the ground arfter me. I knew right then that none a them cucumbers were ever gonna hit me en that they were just landin on the ground all by their lonesome, fallin further en further behind me as I walked away.

Glossary, Bud

Aboat: About (somewheres...where you shouldn't be, most likely)

Boat: About (talkin boat lobsterin weth)

Blapper: Slap shot (sender back for a blapper)

Doon: Doing (how yah doon, a'night?)

En: And (used whin yer talkin like a broken record)

Enna: And a (hed glasses enna sore arse)

Er: Or

Ferr: Feller (Lio Simpson was the worsta them ferrs)

Frig that shit: Nope (frig that shit)

Givver Jimmie: Give her some elbow grease (pull on the Ski-Doo cord)

Hed: Had (hed glasses enna sore arse from some friggen chrome disease)

Henns: Hands (wiped her henns acrost the backa her nose)

His ol scritch wife: His better half (then I seen his ol scritch wife)

How's she hangin? Left er right side, bud?

Innit: In it (innit fer the pardy)

Jest: Just (jest a lazy port rat headed straight fer the vocational school)

Layya: Lay a (layya string a wire oat back)

Moran: More than (moran a month a Sundays)

Nut: Not (four tickets for a ride, nut two)

Oat: Out (oat back, tangled in the wild cucumbers)

Put the blocks to: Have sex with (put the blocks to his wife)

Seen: Seeing (seen as he once tole me)

Sender: Send her (sender back)

Serday: Saturday (beans en weiners night)

Siddown or Set: Sit; sit down (siddown on the rug)

Snubdum: Snubbed him (wandered into the L.C. and snubdum)

Stennin: Standing (a crowda dirty-faced kids stenning overa home plate)

Sumpin: Something (sumpinerudder)

Tell: Till (tell I nearly fell off the pier whin I seen that slimy Safeway bag with dead kittens inside)

Tole: Told (seen as he once tole me)

Wall: While (wall the FerrisWheel Carnie grunted)

Weth: With (weth his ol man in Shelburne)

Whin: When (whin you been cryin, young fullah)

I am grateful to the Ontario Arts Council and The Toronto Arts Council for grants which allowed me time to work on the manuscript. Before I received the grants I was working a door-to-door sales job, and so the money allowed me to quit and to concentrate on the manuscript.

Some of the poems in *Scouts Are Cancelled* have appeared in *The Literary Review of Canada*, *The I.V. Lounge Reader, lichen* and *Another Toronto Quarterly*. The short story "Me and Lio" first appeared in *Pagitica in Toronto*.

The poems are set in the Annapolis Valley but were written in Toronto and first performed at the weekly open mic at the Art Bar Series at The Imperial Library Pub in Toronto. The first journal to accept the poems was *lichen* but the first journal to publish them was *The I.V. Lounge Reader* when Paul Vermeersch told me after a reading, "You're in." The poems have also been read at Shep's grade 12 English class at my high school alma mater, Horton District High School in Nova Scotia and I have stood and subjected the ladies at the Port Williams Women's Institute meeting to a reading. I also performed the poems between sets or as the opening act for gigs with the Corb Lund Band during a 2000 tour of Ontario and Quebec.

I would just like to thank my parents, David and Victoria, my brother and sister, Mark and Susie, for untiring faith and support; Paul, Amy, AJ Levin, Paddy, Carleton, Clink et al; Mike O'Connor, Richard Almonte, Adrienne Weiss (for Ski-Doo and other ms. edits), Jan Barbieri (for "alphabets"), Veridiana, Judgement Day Lund for true friendship; rude word games and rides into Pincher Creek for Slurpees; and my childhood and teenage friends from down the Port where I grew up: Kevin, Greg, Jamie, Stephan, Trevor. I would also like to thank Harry and the 1st Port Williams Scout Troupe and winters at Camp Sasquatch as well as Pat and Blair at the local apple orchard where I picked Cortlands, Russets, Macintosh and Gravensteins with my mum to pay for my first stereo, a tinny sounding number which I loved despite its obvious shortcomings.